OLD ROSES

THE NEW PLANT LIBRARY

OLD ROSES

ANDREW MIKOLAJSKI

Consultant: Lin Hawthorne
Photography by Peter Anderson

LORENZ BOOKS
NEW YORK • LONDON • SYDNEY • BATH

First published in 1997 by Lorenz Books
27 West 20th Street, New York, New York 10011

LORENZ BOOKS are available for bulk purchase for sales promotion and
for premium use. For details, write or call the manager of special sales:
Lorenz Books, 27 West 20th Street, New York, New York 10011;
(212) 807-6739

Lorenz Books is an imprint of
Anness Publishing Limited

ISBN 1 85967 389 9

Publisher: Joanna Lorenz
Editor: Joanna Bentley
Designer: Michael Morey

Printed and bound in Hong Kong

1 3 5 7 9 10 8 6 4 2

Contents

Introduction

*T*he *grandes dames* of the summer border and unsurpassed for their sumptuous flowers and heady fragrance, old roses still do, deservedly, find a place in every garden. That they have endured is a tribute not only to their beauty but also to their ease of cultivation. This book shows you how to grow and care for these marvelous plants as well as illustrating some of their loveliest examples. It also includes some of the species that are the parents of many roses grown in gardens today, as well as some modern hybrids that share the characteristics of the true old roses.

■ RIGHT
The English rose 'Constance Spry' trained against a wall.

The history of old roses

What is an 'old' rose? Some define an old rose as one that was developed and grown before the First World War (1914 – 18), but the answer to this deceptively simple question is unfortunately not quite so clear cut. Indeed, it would be simpler to turn it on its head and ask what a modern rose is. By common consent, modern roses are the large-flowered and cluster-flowered roses (formerly hybrid teas and floribundas) that until recently made up the majority of roses in commerce. Given the fact that the first hybrid tea – 'La France' – appeared as long ago as 1867, it will be evident from the discussion below that many of the so-called old roses are a good deal younger than that.

Nowadays, the long and stately catalogue of old roses comprises various distinct groups: gallicas, damasks, albas, centifolias, mosses, Bourbons, Portlands, Chinas, hybrid perpetuals and teas. In this book we also include the attendant species or wild roses, rugosas, hybrid musks, modern shrub roses and English roses (for descriptions of each see "Classification and flower shapes").

It is probably true to say that for as long as people have made gardens they have grown roses in them; indeed, it would be impossible to exaggerate the rose's importance as the *nonpareil* among garden plants, and its mystique transcends the usual cultural barriers.

Precisely when many of the individual groups arose is not known, but what is certain is that one of the first to be grown in gardens that is recognizable today is *Rosa gallica*. The influence of this rose is present in nearly all of the roses that are still big favorites today. A cross between this and *R. phoenicia* (or possibly *R. moschata*) resulted in *R.* x *damascena*,

■ OPPOSITE

The tall perennial *Campanula lactiflora* blends
happily with many of the old roses. The cultivar
shown here is 'Prichard's Variety'.

■ BELOW

One of the most ancient of roses, 'Old
Blush China' also has one of the longest
flowering seasons.

A moss rose, showing the characteristic mossy stems and calyces.

Constantinople in the 16th century. In medieval Europe, roses came to be associated both with the Holy Spirit and the Virgin Mary. *R. gallica* var. *officinalis* had a commercial value and was known as the apothecary's rose because it was used as an ingredient in medicines, or as the Provins rose after the area of France where it was grown for perfume production.

In England, its flower was adopted as the badge of the House of Lancaster. The rival House of York used 'Alba Semiplena' (or possibly the British native *R. arvensis*), and Henry VII merged the two – heraldically speaking – to form the Tudor rose. Later, the double 'Alba Maxima' became the emblem of Bonnie Prince Charlie.

Botticelli used some artistic license, since the rose is the quintessential flower of summer, when he painted his *Primavera* – she who embodies Spring – wearing a dress decorated with roses; she also carries a bouquet of the same flowers.

Centifolias – sometimes called cabbage roses – were common in Holland and France, to the extent that they were sometimes known as Holland or Provence roses; they often appear in 17th-century Dutch flower paintings.

the original damask. Further crosses and back-crosses occurred, and out of the melting-pot emerged the albas. Pliny the Younger, the great Roman letter writer, grew various kinds at his two country villas, and the Romans introduced some of them into the rest of their Western empire. Pliny also grew a rose he described as centifolia (literally, with a hundred leaves, although meaning petals), but this is thought to be a different rose to the

centifolias we know today. These did not evolve until the 16th century.

The rose retained its supremacy throughout the medieval period and the Renaissance, and acquired both sacred and secular resonances. It was one of the celebrated plants in the gardens of Islam since it was believed to have been created from a bead of perspiration on the brow of Mohammed, and roses are recorded growing in the palace garden in

■ BELOW
Venus, patroness of flower gardens,
oversees a mass planting of roses.

The moss rose, *R.* x *centifolia* 'Muscosa', which is distinguished by its mossy stems and calyces (the green segments that enclose the unopened bud), is a sport (a spontaneous mutation) of a centifolia that was first noticed in approximately 1720. At around the same time, China and tea roses began to arrive in Europe from the Far East. Initially attracting little interest other than as novelties, since they did not prove to be hardy in northern European climates and thus had to be grown under glass, they contributed significantly to the explosion in rose breeding that occurred in the 19th century. Unfortunately, little is known of the history of these plants prior to their European debut.

The value of the tea and China roses as breeding material lay not only in their elegance, scent and color but in the fact that they have an extended

■ BELOW
In late summer, the soft tones of border
phlox blend beautifully with old roses.

■ RIGHT

The hybrid musk rose 'Penelope' in full bloom.

flowering season: Some produce two distinct flushes and others flower virtually non-stop through the summer. Earlier European groups produce one glorious crop of flowers in mid-summer then do not flower again. The so-called autumn damask (*R.* x *damascena* var. *semperflorens*), sometimes called 'Quatre Saisons', is an exception that squeezes out a few more blooms in autumn. Crosses between this and the Chinas resulted in the repeat-flowering Bourbon and Portland roses that became the new stars in the rose firmament. Further crossbreeding led to the hybrid perpetuals, which have a more dependable second flush. All of the modern repeat-flowering roses owe this characteristic to the Chinas.

It was in 19th-century France that rose breeding began in earnest, and it is from this period on that most of the old roses we still grow today were bred. Their names read like a roll call of the top brass and society beauties of the day: the Duc de Guiche, Président de Sèze, the Duchesse de Montebello and Madame Hardy. The vogue was started by the interest, indeed passion, of the Empress Josephine (1763–1814). At her country house of Malmaison she created what was

virtually the first rose garden. Her 250 plants were recorded for posterity by the great botanical artist Pierre-Joseph Redouté. This was probably the rose's heyday – at least before the development of the hybrid teas and floribundas – but a number of mainly English rosarians kept the torch glowing into the 20th century. Among the prime movers were Gertrude Jekyll and the Reverend Joseph Pemberton, who created the

group of roses called hybrid musks, probably by crossing a musk rose with a tea or China rose. Vita Sackville-West grew many old roses in her garden at Sissinghurst and also fostered interest in them through her writings. More recently, David Austin developed a new group that he called English roses, which combine the style of the older groups with the repeat-flowering and robust habit of modern roses.

Old roses in the garden

Generally tough, hardy and free-flowering, old roses are splendid subjects for the garden, and all lend themselves to an informal, mixed, cottage style of planting that uses other shrubs, hardy perennials and summer bulbs. Many make large, rangy plants that may need some form of support (see "Alternative ways of growing old roses"), or you can allow them to flop over gracefully into neighboring shrubs. There are some gallicas, Chinas and teas, however, that grow no larger than 4 feet and are suitable for the smallest gardens.

Flower colors of the European types include white, all shades of pink, dusky red, crimson and purple; some flowers, such as *R. gallica* 'Versicolor' (commonly known as 'Rosa Mundi') and 'Variegata di Bologna' (Bourbon), are striped in a combination of these colors. Genes from the China and tea roses have widened the range to include yellow and soft orange, but on the whole the palette is one that we associate with old silks, chintzes and velvets. In some flowers, the color changes as the flower ages, a good example being the gallica 'Belle de Crécy', whose rich lilac flowers gradually pale into tones of dove gray. On the whole, therefore, it is best to keep old roses away from other flowers that have strong clear colors, though for a bold contrast you could try the rich purple gallicas 'Cardinal de Richelieu' or 'Tuscany Superb' with a sulfur-yellow *Achillea* such as 'Gold Plate'.

Otherwise, for strong contrasts, it is probably better to think in terms of form rather than color. The

■ OPPOSITE

A spectacular massed planting: a vigorous philadelphus forms the backdrop, while a mature Bourbon spreads its arching canes accommodatingly to fill the middle ground. Reliable hardy geraniums and *Dianthus* grow at their feet.

■ LEFT

A ceanothus graciously supports an old rose and a late-flowering clematis.

■ BELOW

The color blue always provides a perfect
foil for soft pink roses such as rosa
'De Meaux'.

geometric shapes of alliums (*A.
sphaerocephalon* or *A. giganteum*) are
the perfect foil to the roses' lax habit,
or try the strong verticals of foxgloves
(*Digitalis purpurea*), in their white or
apricot-pink forms, or the milky-blue
or white Canterbury bells

(*Campanula medium*), both biennials
that are easily raised from seed. The
perennial *C. lactiflora* would also
work well, particularly the dusky pink
variety 'Loddon Anna'.

For a less spiky, more integrated
effect use easy border perennials, such

as hardy geraniums, lady's mantle
(*Alchemilla mollis*) or catmint (*Nepeta
x faassenii*), all of which will blend
with most old roses. Clouds of
gypsophila (*G. paniculata*) or bronze
fennel (*Foeniculum vulgare* 'Purpureum')
will further soften the edges.

■ RIGHT

The flagon-shaped, vibrant red hips of *R. moyesii* make a stunning clash with purple *Thalictrum aquilegiifolium*.

If you are still concerned about color clashes, add a few gray-leaved plants such as artemisia (especially *A. lactiflora*), lambs' ears (*Stachys byzantina*), sage (*Salvia officinalis*) or *Senecio* (now sometimes listed as *Brachyglottis*) 'Sunshine', though you will have to remove its ugly daisy-like flowers. In a large border, underplant a tall-growing rose such as the alba 'Great Maiden's Blush' with a hosta. The huge leaves of *H. sieboldiana* 'Elegans' would provide a sumptuous quilted cushion for the roses to rest on. For edging, tightly clipped box (*Buxus sempervirens* 'Suffruticosa') is traditional, but lavender, rosemary or the curry plant (*Helichrysum italicum*) would be more informal.

Besides the beauty of the flowers, and perhaps even above that, roses are prized for their scent. This can range from the delicate tang of a modern shrub such as 'Nevada', more apparent wafted on the air from a distance than close to, to the rich, crushed-berry fragrance of the Bourbon 'Madame Isaac Pereire'.

To create a voluptuous potpourri of scents, provide a backdrop of mock orange (*Philadelphus*), the flowering of which will coincide with the roses' early summer flush. Underplant with old-fashioned pinks (*Dianthus*), such as the clove-scented 'Gran's Favourite' or 'Sops-in-Wine', the headily fragrant lily *Lilium regale* or the incense-scented annual tobacco flower, *Nicotiana alata*. Remember that the scents will be heaviest at dusk, particularly after a light shower.

If your roses are the kind that produce a single crop of flowers, for interest later in the season use them as props for late-flowering clematis.

The rich purple 'Jackmanii', one of the most reliable, would look stunning entwined with the vibrant red hips of *R. moyesii* or any of the rugosas, particularly if the flame-red *Crocosmia* 'Lucifer', cannas, dahlias and orange annual nasturtiums (*Tropaeolum majus*) were planted as a supporting cast, bringing the curtain down on the rose season with a sensational chorus of color.

Classification and flower shapes

When attempting to classify old roses, there is no hard-and-fast rule: Even the term old rose itself is misleading, and included here are some modern hybrids that have the grace and flower form of older roses. The categories described here are broadly accepted by the rose-growing community, but there will always be a few plants included in one group that some growers may feel belong rightly in one of the others.

Wild

This group includes the species and those roses that are selections of them. They generally produce one flush of single flowers in early summer, and often have decorative hips.

Alba

Large, strong-growing roses with attractive gray-green foliage that produce a single flush of white or pale pink flowers in mid-summer.

Bourbon and Portland

Bourbons are vigorous roses, usually repeat-flowering, that can also be trained as short climbers, derived from a damask/China cross. Portland roses, resulting from a damask/gallica cross, are similar but repeat more reliably and make smaller plants.

Centifolia and moss

Centifolias make lax shrubs with large, many-petalled flowers that weigh down the arching canes. The leaves are large, drooping and sometimes wrinkled. Centifolias are sometimes referred to as cabbage, Provence or Holland roses. Moss roses are a closely allied group, arising as sports of centifolias and damasks, but are distinguished by the characteristic mossy growth on their stems and calyces.

China and tea

China roses are dainty, repeat-flowering shrubs of light, open habit with small, scented flowers and leaves. A few are grown under glass in

■ OPPOSITE

The tomato-red hips of *R. rugosa* are as decorative as the flowers.

■ BELOW

The wild rose 'Andersonii' makes a large shrub that smothers itself in flowers in early summer.

cold climates, since they are not fully hardy. Tea roses are slender-stemmed, repeat-flowering, often weak-growing shrubs, some of which need glass-house protection in cold climates. Slender, pointed buds are a feature of many of the modern, large-flowered roses that are derived from them and are often known as hybrid teas.

Damask

Lax, spreading, medium-size to large shrubs, usually with highly scented flowers in clear colors. The leaves are typically grayish-green and are downy underneath.

Gallica

Usually upright, though sometimes spreading, compact shrubs with coarse leaves and flowers in deep shades of pink, rich crimson and purple. The group includes some striped roses.

Hybrid perpetual

Vigorous shrubs, usually repeat-flowering, that initially grow upright. Legginess tends to develop later, a problem that can be overcome by pegging down the overlong shoots.

Other types

Rugosa roses are tough, vigorous, very hardy plants with crinkled foliage and single to double flowers that are succeeded by large, tomato-like hips. They originated in the Far East and have not been used extensively in rose breeding in the West but are easy to grow and are valued for their robust constitution.

Scotch roses are dense shrubs with *R. pimpinellifolia* (the Scotch or Burnet rose) in their make-up.

Modern shrub roses are usually large, repeat-flowering shrubs that were bred after the advent of large-flowered and cluster-flowered roses. Hybrid musks are similar, but have the musk rose (*R. moschata*) in their pedigree.

Polyanthus are now more or less obsolete. They are tough and repeat-flowering and produce trusses of small flowers; these are the forebears of the modern cluster-flowered roses.

So-called English roses were developed from the late 1950s onward by the rose-breeder David Austin with the intention of combining the flower types found in old roses with the repeat-flowering habit of large-flowered and cluster-flowered roses.

■ BELOW – LEFT TO RIGHT

Flower shapes: rosette, quartered rosette and pompon.

■ BOTTOM

Flower shapes left to right: urn-shaped and pointed.

Flower shapes

Flat

Single (with five petals) or semi-double (with ten petals) flowers that open virtually flat, often revealing prominent stamens.

Cupped

Single to fully double flowers with curving petals forming a shallow to deep cup shape.

Pointed and urn-shaped

The characteristic shape of China and tea roses; the long, slender, elegant buds opening to high-centered, pointed or urn-shaped flowers.

Rounded

Flowers with a rounded outline, formed by overlapping petals, usually of equal size.

Rosette

Low-centered, flat flowers with many short, crowded petals.

Quartered rosette

Similar to rosette, but with the petals arranged in distinctive quarters.

Pompon

Small, ball-like flowers, generally borne in clusters, with many short petals.

x

x

Plant Catalog

In the following gallery, roses are arranged alphabetically within categories as follows (for further information, see "Classification and flower shapes").

Wild roses
Albas
Bourbons
Centifolias and mosses
Chinas and teas
Damasks
Gallicas
Other types

The height and spread cited are what the rose can be expected to achieve on maturity; they may vary depending on climate, season and soil type.

■ ABOVE
R. XANTHINA 'CANARY BIRD'

Wild rose of uncertain origin but assumed to be after 1907, the date of introduction of one of its possible parents, *R. xanthina* f. *spontanea*. It makes an arching shrub, 7 feet high and as much across or bigger. In late spring, the canes are covered in cupped, single, scented, canary-yellow flowers with prominent stamens. The leaves are fern-like. *R. xanthina* 'Canary Bird', one of the earliest roses to flower, tolerates some shade. It is sometimes available as a grafted standard.

Wild roses

■ RIGHT
'DUPONTII'

Wild rose hybrid, introduced around 1817, that forms a spreading shrub 7 feet high and across. In summer, the large, single, creamy white flowers open flat to reveal yellow stamens. The matte gray-green leaves are downy beneath. 'Dupontii' was grown by Empress Josephine and illustrated by Redouté as *R. damascena subalba*.

Albas

■ BELOW
'ALBA MAXIMA'

Alba rose, dating from at least the 15th century, reaching a height of 6 feet with a spread of 5 feet. Somewhat untidy, cupped, double, very fragrant flowers, tinged pink on opening in summer but fading to creamy white, are followed by red hips. The foliage is lead-green. A rose of great historical significance, 'Alba Maxima' is sometimes known as the Great White, Jacobite or Cheshire rose, while others consider it to be the White Rose of York (see also 'Alba Semiplena').

■ LEFT
'ALBA SEMIPLENA'

Alba rose, known in gardens since at least the 16th century. It is a graceful shrub with a height of 6 feet and a spread of 5 feet. In summer, clusters of semi-double, very fragrant, milky-white flowers open flat to display prominent golden stamens. Red hips form in late summer to autumn. 'Alba Semiplena' is usually held to be the White Rose of York (see also 'Alba Maxima').

'CELESTE'

Alba rose with a lax and spreading habit that produces a shrub 6 feet high and across, or more. The semi-double, sweetly scented, shell-pink flowers, with petals that appear almost transparent, are borne in summer and open flat to reveal prominent golden stamens. Red hips succeed them in autumn. The leaves are gray-green. The date of introduction of 'Céleste' is unrecorded, but it is certainly a very old cultivar. It is sometimes listed as 'Celestial'.

■ ABOVE
'FELICITE PARMENTIER'

Alba rose, known since about 1834, that grows into a compact shrub 4 feet high and across. In midsummer, it bears clusters of cup-shaped, highly scented, quartered, pale blush-pink flowers that open from primrose-yellow buds. The densely packed petals fade to almost white in hot sun and reflex to form a ball-shape. The leaves are gray-green. One of the daintiest of the albas, 'Félicité Parmentier' would suit the smallest garden.

■ ABOVE
'KONIGIN VON DANEMARK'

Alba rose, produced in 1826, that makes a tall, elegant bush up to 5 feet high and 4 feet across. The luminous pink flowers, borne in summer, are fully double, quartered rosette and richly scented, the color fading to rose-pink as they mature. The leaves are pale grayish-green. 'Königin von Dänemark', sometimes sold as 'Queen of Denmark', has one of the longest flowering seasons – up to six weeks – and the flowers have good resistance to wet weather.

Bourbons

■ RIGHT
'LOUISE ODIER'

Bourbon rose, introduced in 1851, that makes a shrub 4 feet high and across. From mid-summer to autumn, it produces cupped, fully double, strongly scented, lilac-tinted, warm-pink flowers. The leaves are light gray-green. 'Louise Odier' has slender shoots that can be supported on a pillar or tripod.

■ LEFT
'BOULE DE NEIGE'

Bourbon rose, introduced in 1867, growing to 5 feet high and 4 feet across, though the weight of the flowers may pull the slender stems further sideways; hence it is best with some support. In summer and autumn, clusters of red-tinted buds open to fully double, deeply cupped, strongly scented, white flowers. The leaves are leathery and dark green. 'Boule de Neige' (snowball) is so named because as the flowers develop the petals curl back to produce a ball shape.

■ RIGHT
'HONORINE DE BRABANT'

Bourbon rose, of unknown origin, that grows into a shrub about 6 feet high and across. Its cupped, fully double, strongly but sweetly scented flowers are borne continuously from summer through to autumn, the autumn flowering being particularly good; the petals are pale pink, spotted and striped with mauve and crimson. The leaves are large and light green. 'Honorine de Brabant' tolerates poor soil; a sprawling rose, it is best with some support and may be trained as a short climber.

■ BELOW
'BLAIRII NUMBER TWO'

Bourbon rose raised in 1845, that, if untrained, will grow into an arching shrub 7 feet high and across or more. An abundance of large, cupped, fully double, sweetly scented flowers in mid-summer are pale silvery pink with deeper pink centers. The leaves, rough to the touch, are matte dark green. 'Blairii Number Two' produces few, if any, further blooms in autumn. Its rigor makes it suitable for growing as a pyramid, on a pergola or against a wall, where it can reach 15 feet.

■ LEFT
'SOUVENIR DE LA MALMAISON'

Bourbon rose, produced in 1843, growing into a dense shrub 5 feet high and across. Repeating throughout summer, it bears very fragrant, fully double, soft pink flowers that open to a quartered-rosette shape as they fade to pinkish-white. The leaves are large. 'Souvenir de la Malmaison' is named in honor of Empress Josephine's famous garden at Malmaison; the silk-textured flowers may be spoiled by wet weather.

■ RIGHT
'MADAME ISAAC PEREIRE'

Bourbon rose, introduced in 1881, that grows into a large plant up to 7 feet high and 6 feet across. Borne from summer to autumn, the huge, richly fragrant, luminous deep cerise-pink flowers open as quartered rosettes but become muddled as they mature, especially those of the first flush. The matte dark green leaves are abundant. 'Madame Isaac Pereire', one of the most strongly scented of all roses, is a vigorous plant that can also be trained as a climber.

Centifolias and mosses

■ RIGHT
'CHAPEAU DE NAPOLEON'

Centifolia rose, bred in the 1820s. It is
sometimes incorrectly included among the moss
roses. It makes a graceful, slender-stemmed
shrub 5 feet high and 4 feet across. In summer,
it produces drooping, cupped, fully double,
richly scented, deep silvery pink flowers that
open flat and are sometimes quartered. The
foliage is abundant. 'Chapeau de Napoléon' is
now more correctly known as *R.* x *centifolia*
'Cristata'. The name 'Chapeau de Napoléon'
refers to the unopened buds (see inset), which
are three-cornered like the tricorn hat
characteristically worn by Napoleon.

■ LEFT
'FANTIN-LATOUR'

Centifolia rose, dating from around 1900,
that makes a handsome, vase-shaped shrub
up to 7 feet high and across. The flowers –
cup-shaped, many-petalled, delicately
scented and blush-pink – are borne in
profusion over a long period in summer.
The petals reflex to reveal a green button
eye. The leaves are dark green. 'Fantin-
Latour' was named in honor of the French
flower painter Henri Fantin-Latour
(1836–1904). Spraying against mildew
may be necessary in summer.

■ LEFT
'NUITS DE YOUNG'

Moss rose, dating from 1845, that forms an upright, then arching, shrub 4 feet high and 3 feet across. Small, double, lightly scented, maroon-purple flowers open flat in summer to reveal golden stamens. The leaves are small and dark green. 'Nuits de Young' is valued for its unique dusky coloring; even the mossing of the stems and buds is dark reddish-brown. Its other name, appropriately, is 'Old Black'.

■ RIGHT
'WILLIAM LOBB'

Moss rose, introduced in 1855, that makes an upright but sprawling shrub 6 feet high and across. In midsummer the large, double, rosette, heavily scented, magenta-purple flowers open from heavily mossed buds then fade to violet-gray. The dark green leaves are abundant. 'William Lobb' is a vigorous rose that benefits from some support; it can be trained as a short climber on a pillar or against a wall. The tonal range of the flowers as they mature and fade is remarkable.

Chinas and teas

'CECILE BRUNNER'

China rose, sometimes classified as a polyanthus, introduced in 1880, that makes a dainty bush about 3 feet high and across. From summer to autumn, clusters of pointed buds open to urn-shaped, delicately scented, pale pink flowers that become more untidy as they age. The leaves are pointed and sparse. The buds are good for buttonholes, which may explain the common name, Sweetheart rose. Occasionally listed as 'Mignon', 'Cécile Brünner' is also sometimes known as the Maltese rose. A climbing form is available, and a rare white-flowered form.

R. ODORATA 'MUTABILIS'

China rose, of uncertain parentage, introduced from China before 1894. It makes a strong shrub about 3 to 6 feet high and across. The single, cupped, lightly scented flowers, borne through summer to autumn, are of unique coloring. Flame orange in bud, they open to coppery yellow then fade to pink, deepening to purple as they age. The leaves are dark green and glossy. *R. odorata* 'Mutabilis' (sometimes sold as *R. chinensis* 'Mutabilis' or simply 'Mutabilis') appreciates a warm site against a wall; grown as a climber, it can reach a height of 8 feet or more.

Damasks

■ RIGHT
'ISPAHAN'

Damask rose, first recorded in 1832 but probably much older; it may be Persian in origin. It makes a compact shrub with a height of 4 to 5 feet and a spread of 3 to 4 feet. Large clusters of cupped, loosely double, reflexing, richly scented, clear pink flowers appear in summer. The gray-green foliage is attractive. 'Ispahan' has a longer flowering season than most other damasks and is in bloom for up to six weeks.

■ LEFT
'MADAME HARDY'

Damask rose, dating from 1867, that makes an elegant shrub up to 5 feet high and across. Cupped, fully double, quartered-rosette, strongly scented white flowers are borne in profusion in summer, the petals reflexing to reveal a green button eye. The foliage is plentiful and matte light green. 'Madame Hardy' is generally considered to be one of the most sumptuous of old roses, though the flowers may be spoiled by rain.

Gallicas

■ RIGHT

'BELLE DE CRECY'

Gallica rose, bred before 1829, making a
bush about 4 feet high and 3 feet across.
The quartered rosettes of sweetly scented
flowers, produced in abundance in
midsummer, open rich lilac-pink then fade
to paler pink. The leaves are dull green.
'Belle de Crécy', though one of the best
gallicas, has a laxer habit than most and its
arching stems may require support.

■ LEFT

'CHARLES DE MILLS'

Gallica rose that makes a compact shrub up to 4 feet in height with a spread of 3 feet or more. The fully double, quartered-rosette, moderately scented, rich crimson flowers, which are produced in summer, fade with gray and purple tones as they mature. The abundant foliage is matte dark green. 'Charles de Mills', sometimes sold as 'Bizarre Triomphant', has slender stems that may need staking to support the large flowers. Its parentage and date of introduction are unknown.

■ OPPOSITE

'CARDINAL DE RICHELIEU'

Gallica rose, produced in 1840, that makes a compact bush 4 feet high and across, more if the stems are supported. In midsummer it bears clusters of sumptuous, scented, dark maroon flowers, the petals of which are velvety in texture and reflex as the flowers age to form a ball shape. The stems are well covered with dark green leaves. 'Cardinal de Richelieu' needs good growing conditions and regular thinning of the old wood to give of its best. It can be used for hedging.

■ LEFT

'COMPLICATA'

Gallica rose that, as a free-standing shrub, grows to 8 feet high and wide. The single, cupped, sweetly scented flowers, produced in abundance in summer, are bright porcelain-pink and open wide to reveal white centers and golden stamens. The leaves are matte grayish-green and, unusually for a gallica, rather pointed. 'Complicata' is not typical of its group and is of uncertain origin. It can be used as a rambler among trees and shrubs in a wild garden or can be trained on a pillar; it tolerates light, sandy soils.

■ LEFT
'DUCHESSE DE MONTEBELLO'

Gallica rose, bred before 1829, that makes
a spreading bush about 4 feet high and
across. The open-cupped, fully double,
sweetly fragrant flowers are soft blush-
pink. The foliage is light green. 'Duchesse
de Montebello' is one of the daintiest and
neatest-growing of the gallicas.

■ ABOVE RIGHT
'DU MAITRE D'ECOLE'

Gallica rose that makes a compact plant
about 3 feet high and across, wider in
summer when the weight of blossom
makes the stems arch over. The fully
double, quartered-rosette, carmine-pink
flowers open flat and fade to lilac-pink and
gray. The dense, matte mid-green foliage is
abundant. The date of introduction of 'Du
Maître d'Ecole' is debated but is said by
some authorities to be 1840.

■ RIGHT
'DUC DE GUICHE'

Gallica rose that forms a shrub 4 feet high
and across. In summer, it produces large,
fully double, highly scented, rich crimson
flowers; as they age, the petals develop
purple veining, the flowers finally flushing
purple. The leaves are matte dark green.
'Duc de Guiche', an outstanding gallica, is
of uncertain origin and date.

■ RIGHT

R. GALLICA VAR. *OFFICINALIS*

Gallica rose, recorded in gardens since
the 13th century, it makes a bushy shrub
up to 4 feet high and across. In summer,
it produces an abundance of large,
semidouble, sweetly fragrant, light crimson
flowers that open flat and reveal golden
stamens. The leaves are coarse. *R. gallica*
var. *officinalis* is a superb garden plant that
is rich in historical associations both as the
Red Rose of Lancaster and the medieval
apothecary's rose.

■ LEFT

'PRESIDENT DE SEZE'

Gallica rose, introduced before 1836, that
grows into a sturdy shrub 4 feet high by
3 feet across. In summer, it produces
large, quartered, richly scented flowers; the
center petals are rich magenta-purple, the
color fading across the flower to soft
lilac-pink, almost white, at the edges. The
leaves are larger than is usual for a
gallica. A well-grown specimen of
'Président de Sèze' is a remarkable sight
when in full bloom.

■ LEFT
'TUSCANY SUPERB'

Gallica rose, raised before 1837, making an erect shrub 5 feet high and 3 feet across. The large, semi-double, lightly scented, deep crimson flowers, produced in midsummer, open flat, showing golden stamens, then fade to purple. The foliage is abundant. Tolerant of poor soil, 'Tuscany Superb' may be used for hedging; it richly deserves its other name, 'Double Velvet'.

■ LEFT
R. GALLICA 'VERSICOLOR'

Gallica rose, recorded in the 16th century but probably much older. It makes a neat shrub up to 4 feet high and across. The lightly scented flowers, produced in midsummer, are semidouble, opening flat to reveal golden stamens. The petals are pale pink, splashed and striped with red and crimson. The leaves are dull mid-green. *R. gallica* 'Versicolor' is commonly known as 'Rosa Mundi', after Fair Rosamund, the mistress of Henry II of England.

Other types

'BUFF BEAUTY'

Modern shrub rose, sometimes classified as
a hybrid musk, bred probably before 1939.
It grows to about 5 feet high and across.
The cupped, fully double, sweetly scented,
pale buff-apricot flowers are carried in
clusters in two flushes, the autumn
flowering being less profuse. The leaves are
tinged reddish-purple when young,
turning dark green. 'Buff Beauty' can be
used for hedging but, with the weight of
the flowers on the canes, may need the
support of horizontal wires. Mildew
may be a problem in late summer.

'CONSTANCE SPRY'

Modern shrub, sometimes classified as an
'English' rose, though it flowers once only,
in summer. Introduced in 1961, untrained
it makes a large, lax shrub up to 6 feet
high and across. The large, cupped, fully
double, peony-like flowers are rich pink
and heavily scented. The abundant leaves
are dull green. 'Constance Spry' can also be
grown as a climber on a pillar, or will
tolerate shade against a wall. As a shrub it
is best given some support or pruned hard
to keep it compact.

■ RIGHT

'FRUHLINGSGOLD'

Scotch hybrid rose, sometimes classified as a modern shrub rose, introduced in 1937. It makes a vigorous shrub, each arching cane reaching up to 7 feet long. The large, cupped, semidouble, fragrant, primrose-yellow flowers cover the canes in late spring to early summer. The flowers open flat from long, pointed buds to display golden stamens. The long green leaves are pointed. 'Frühlingsgold' is a tough, thorny plant that would be excellent planted as a barrier.

■ LEFT

'GRAHAM THOMAS'

Modern shrub or 'English' rose, introduced in 1983, that forms a vigorous shrub 4 to 8 feet high with a similar spread. The flowers, produced from summer to autumn, are cupped, fully double, fragrant and rich yellow. The leaves are glossy. Named in honor of the great English rosarian, Graham Stuart Thomas, 'Graham Thomas' was considered a notable introduction, since yellow is virtually absent among true old roses.

■ RIGHT

'GRUSS AN AACHEN'

Modern rose, usually classified as a cluster-flowered bush. It was bred around 1909 and makes a bush up to 5 feet high and across. The shapely, deeply cupped, fully double, delicately scented flowers are tinged pink on opening, then fade to creamy white, and are carried in clusters from summer to autumn. The leaves are dark green and leathery. Its long flowering season and low habit of growth make 'Gruss an Aachen' an outstanding bedding rose.

■ RIGHT

'ROSERAIE DE L'HAY'

Rugosa rose, introduced in 1901, that makes a dense shrub up to 7 feet high and across. The flowers are borne continuously through summer and into autumn. They are cupped (opening flat to reveal creamy stamens), fully double, heavily scented and rich wine-red. Few autumn hips are produced. The leaves are crinkled and bright green. 'Roseraie de l'Haÿ' is weather-resistant and makes a splendid hedge; since it tolerates poor soil and some shade, it can also be planted in light woodland.

■ *ABOVE*

'STANWELL PERPETUAL'

Scotch rose, introduced in 1838, that forms a dense, prickly shrub that can reach 5 feet high and across. The double, sweetly scented, blush-pink to white flowers that open flat are produced almost continuously throughout the summer. The leaves are gray-green. 'Stanwell Perpetual' tolerates poor soil and some shade, so may be planted in woodland; it also makes a good hedge.

Cultivation

Roses will tolerate most soil types, except soil that is permanently wet, but the ideal is an easily workable loam (made up of roughly equal parts of sand, silt and clay) that is rich in humus (decayed vegetable matter). Roses are said to prefer heavy clay soils that retain nutrients well, but good results can be achieved on thin, alkaline soil, provided you improve it before planting and mulch the plants annually. Adding organic matter in the form of farmyard manure or garden compost improves all soil types, helping to aerate heavy soils and adding bulk and nutrients to light soils. If you have a very heavy soil, working in horticultural grit at the rate of a bucketful per square yard will improve drainage.

Most roses grow best in full sun but with some protection from wind;

■ BELOW
Rosa moyesii, planted among salvias and edged with box, provides a stunning display in late summer.

■ RIGHT
The Bourbon rose 'Ferdinand Pichard'
trained to a stake.

very exposed sites are suitable only for
the tough rugosas. A few tolerate
dappled shade, though growth and
flowering will be less vigorous. No
rose will perform well in deep shade.
Good air circulation around the
plants is important and lessens the
likelihood of mildew and other fungal
diseases (see "Pests, diseases and other
disorders"). Planting them too close
to other shrubs will also limit the
available moisture and nutrients.

For the best results, you need to
feed your roses regularly. Whether
you use organic or inorganic
fertilizers is a matter of personal
choice, but by using chemical
fertilizers you know exactly how
much of the nutrient elements you
are applying. Nitrogen (N)
stimulates lush, leafy growth,
potassium (K) promotes flower
production, and phosphorus (P) aids
root development. 'Balanced' fertilizers
('straights') contain equal amounts of
each, but for optimum performance
use a commercial rose fertilizer that
has a higher proportion of potassium.
Organic gardeners could substitute
pelleted chicken manure.

Fork the fertilizer into the soil
around the base of the plant at the
rate recommended by the manufacturer when growth begins in

spring. Water the fertilizer in well,
then apply a mulch to retain
moisture. On repeat-flowering roses,
you should feed again in midsummer
directly after deadheading (see
"Pruning: summer pruning"), but do
not feed after this, since you will
encourage lush growth that will not
have time to ripen fully before winter.
Forking in a handful of bonemeal
around the base of the plant in
autumn, however, promotes strong

root growth (roots continue to grow
even though top-growth has ceased).

If you need to replace a rose, the
newcomer may not thrive in the same
soil, even if the old one was growing
strongly (see "Pests, diseases and
other disorders: rose-sick soil").
When removing the old plant, dig
out a hole about 3 feet across and 18
inches deep and replace the old soil
with fresh soil that has not already
had roses growing in it.

Buying roses

Roses are sold either as container-grown or bare-root plants (which have been lifted from the open ground while dormant and the roots shaken free of soil). Bare-root plants are usually available only between autumn and early spring. Most growers who sell by mail order supply their plants this way. Although there may be a delay between ordering your plants and delivery, a huge range is available to you.

Garden centers, however, usually prefer to sell plants that are in full growth in containers, but only the most popular varieties are likely to be offered.

Bare-root roses must be planted in autumn or spring. Container-grown roses, although more expensive, can be planted at any time of year except when the ground is frozen or water-logged or during periods of drought. If you plant in late spring or summer months, you will need to water the plants thoroughly in dry weather until they are established.

Good soil preparation prior to planting is essential if the rose is to perform as it should and will considerably minimize maintenance of the plants later on.

PLANTING A CONTAINER-GROWN ROSE

1 Fork over the site to break up and aerate the soil. Remove all weeds, especially perennials such as couch grass and ground elder; fork in organic matter at about the rate of one bucketful per square yard. Then, dig a hole approximately twice the width and depth of the pot.

2 Remove the rose from its pot, trim any damaged roots, and position it in the hole. Check the planting depth with a cane laid across the hole. The graft union (where the rose is budded on the rootstock) should be about 1 inch below soil level.

3 Backfill with soil and firm in with your foot. Fork in rose fertilizer around the base of the plant at the rate recommended by the manufacturer, then water in thoroughly.

4 Mulch with more organic matter to reduce water evaporation from around the base of the plant.

By the end of its first season, a newly planted rose should have made good growth and may even flower.

Planting a bare-root rose

Bare-root roses supplied through the mail are usually shipped in special padded containers. If the conditions are unsuitable for planting when you receive them, you can store them unopened for up to six weeks in a dark, cool place. The roots are usually wrapped in a plastic bag containing peat or some similar material to keep them moist.

PLANTING A BARE-ROOT ROSE

Soak the rose roots in water for about an hour. With sharp pruners, shorten any overlong or damaged roots and remove any dead wood, then follow the procedure recommended for planting a container-grown rose, digging a hole large enough to accommodate the rose's root system.

Planting a container-grown rose

When buying an old rose in a container, look for a specimen that is growing strongly and evenly with sturdy, well-spaced stems. Make sure the plant is free from disease and pests. Check that it is not pot-bound by sliding the plant from its container. If the roots are congested and coil around the inside of the container, they will probably continue to grow in a spiral, and the plant will be slow to establish. The presence of a few weed seedlings on the surface of the soil mix is of no consequence, but a mat of liverworts or mosses indicates that the plant has been in its pot too long.

Planting old roses in containers

Old roses can be successfully grown in containers provided the container is large enough to accommodate the rose's root run. Decide on the final position before you begin planting, because the container will be very heavy to move when it is finished. The rose will probably be in the container for several years, so it is worthwhile spending time on the planting. A layer of stones or gravel in the base of the pot is important both for drainage and to counterbalance the weight of the fully grown rose and prevent it from blowing over in strong winds.

The container used here is a modern reproduction of a classic design believed to be by the great English garden designer Gertrude Jekyll. For a more rustic look, a half barrel would make a less expensive alternative; plastic pots are lighter and therefore less stable, especially for a large plant, but could be used for one of the dainty tea or China roses, particularly if grown under glass, where wind would not be a problem. Plastic pots also have an advantage in that they need watering less often. To maintain vigor in subsequent years top-dress with bonemeal or work in rose fertilizer at the rate recommended by the manufacturer.

The dainty China rose 'Cécile Brünner' planted in a stylish galvanized metal container.

PLANTING A CONTAINER-GROWN ROSE

1 Fill one-third of the pot with gravel. Use loam-based soil mix or an equal mix of loam-based potting soil mix and garden compost to fill the pot deep enough to support the root ball. Wearing gloves, work in a handful of bonemeal.

2 Check the planting depth. You need a gap of about 1 inch between the rim of the container and the top surface of the soil mix to allow for watering.

3 Remove the rose from its pot and gently loosen the roots with a hand fork. This will help the plant to establish more quickly.

4 Backfill with more soil mix and firm in with your hands. Make sure the graft union between the top-growth and the rootstock is covered.

5 Water the plant thoroughly.

6 Top-dress with grit to help keep the roots cool and to prevent excessive evaporation of moisture from the top of the soil mix.

Alternative ways of growing old roses

Though all old roses make excellent border plants, blending easily with a range of other flowers, there are a few that may be grown in other ways, often to their advantage. For instance, you can use them to make an attractive summer-flowering hedge, though since they are not evergreen they cannot be used to make a permanent barrier. All the rugosas are suitable for this purpose, as well as some from the other groups. Plant the roses about 3 feet apart, more if they have a wide spread. Hybrid musks, like 'Buff Beauty', which have a spread that exceeds their height, are best tied to horizontal wires. Most hedges are pruned in summer after flowering by shearing them back to the desired height. Pruning a rugosa hedge then would deprive you of the ornamental hips, so do no more than tidy up the plants in late winter.

Some old roses (hybrid perpetuals, most of the Bourbons and some modern shrubs) produce a quantity of vigorous but flexible stems from near the base of the plant after flowering, and you can take advantage of this habit to enhance the next year's flowering display. Such stems tend to grow upright, then arch over, and will flower only at their tips, but by bringing them down virtually to the

PEGGING DOWN

Bring a vigorous but flexible stem down to as near ground level as possible and peg it to the ground with lengths of wire bent over into hairpin shapes.

This rose, 'Chianti', has been tied to horizontal wires pinned to stakes about 12 inches high. Notice how flowering laterals have been produced all along the length of the stem.

horizontal you will encourage them to produce flowering laterals, particularly on the curve, where growth hormones will accumulate. Using this technique, you can train the plant as a short climber, either against a wall (on a trellis or on horizontal wires) or on a tripod or pergola. For the most dramatic effect, bring the stems down to as near ground level as possible to create a flowering 'table' (a technique usually called 'pegging down'). For a crinoline-like mound of flowers, cut lengths of hazel, or some other flexible wood, insert one end in the ground near the base of the rose, then bend it into a hoop. Tie the rose canes to this as they grow.

If you live in an area that has cold winters, you can grow some of the Chinas that will withstand only a few degrees of frost against a warm wall. In summer, the extra heat reflected by the wall will help to ripen the stems so they are better able to withstand low temperatures. Tie them to a trellis or horizontal wires, training vigorous stems as near to the horizontal as possible. In this way, a China will grow to twice the height it would in the open, but you cannot cover a whole wall with flowers as you can with a true climbing rose.

■ ABOVE LEFT
The Bourbon rose
'Blairii Number
Two' trained on a
pyramid.

■ ABOVE RIGHT
The spread of this
alba rose has been
restricted by tying
the stems to
upright canes.

■ RIGHT
The China rose
'Cécile Brünner'
trained against a
wall.

Pruning

Most old roses are best left to develop to their full potential with minimal pruning, and the annual, rigorous prune demanded by modern roses is not necessary. However, check plants early in the season, as some pruning may be beneficial. For the general well-being of the plant, you should remove any dead, diseased or damaged material and also cut back any branches that cross and rub against each other. Left unpruned, these may damage each other's bark and produce an entry point for disease. It is easiest to prune in early spring, when the branches are still relatively bare, and you can identify which wood needs to be removed and gain easier access to the base of the plant. It is also possible to prune roses that do not repeat flower immediately after flowering (see "Summer pruning," opposite).

Pruning always stimulates vigorous new growth: Pruning too early in the season will encourage the production of fresh green shoots that may succumb to late frosts. This does no lasting harm to the plant, but necessitates further pruning to remove the frosted growth and may check the development of the plant. Since pruning stimulates vigorous growth, lightly prune stems that are

1 In early spring, cut out all dead growth, to the base of the plant if necessary. Also remove any crossing stems that rub against each other.

2 Cut back any other dead wood as far as live material.

3 Shorten laterals by between one-third to a half if necessary. Cut back to a strong bud facing in the direction you wish the stem to grow. Shorten any overlong or badly placed stems by one-third to a half.

already growing quite strongly. Conversely, cut back weak stems hard to encourage strong growth. New growth will always arise from the point at which you cut, so to produce an open, vase-shaped plant, cut just

above an outward-facing bud. Cutting to inward-facing buds will result in congested growth at the heart of the plant that will not flower well. Always use clean, sharp tools. Blunt blades will snag the wood,

providing an entry point for disease.
Wear gloves to protect your hands.

After pruning, feed the plants well,
water and mulch with farmyard
manure, bark chippings or garden
compost. If the rose does not produce
ornamental hips, deadhead after
flowering. This is essential for those
plants that produce a second crop of
flowers. Feed again.

Summer pruning

Unless the rose is grown for its
ornamental hips as well as for its
flowers (e.g. *R. moyesii*), you need to
prune in midsummer after flowering.
Summer pruning has several benefits.
On roses that flower only once, it
makes room for new growth that will
flower freely the following year, and
ensure that it has time to ripen fully
before the winter; on roses that flower
again later in the season, it
encourages a better second crop.
Removing the spent flowers (deadheading) also improves the overall
appearance of the plant.

Gallicas tend to produce a mass of
twiggy shoots that can become
congested. Thin the shoots
periodically throughout the summer.
This will minimize the risk of disease
by improving air circulation.

■ ABOVE
On a pegged-
down rose (or rose
trained as a
climber) shorten
the flowering
laterals to 2–4 sets
of leaves.

■ LEFT
Remove faded
flowers or flower
clusters, cutting
just above the
nearest leaf joint.

Propagation

There are two main methods of increasing your stock of old roses. Budding is a nurseryman's technique, widely practiced within the trade, since saleable plants can be produced quickly this way. Taking cuttings is a simpler but slower method, preferred by amateur gardeners.

Budding

Since most roses are highly bred plants that have lost some of their vigor in the selection process, they are normally propagated by grafting buds onto strong-growing rootstocks, usually of species such as *R. multiflora* or *R. canina*. Because the latter is prone to produce suckers (shoots from below ground level), its selected form 'Laxa', which does not have this fault, is now generally preferred.

Rootstocks are not generally available to the public, so if you wish to increase your stock this way you need to contact a local rose grower and ask if you can buy a rootstock. Patient gardeners can also raise their own stocks from seed.

Budding is usually carried out from midsummer onwards while the plants are still growing. You are more likely to be successful if you choose a wet day, when there is less risk of the propagating material drying out.

Select strong, healthy, well-ripened non-flowering stems from the parent plant. To test for ripeness, bend one of the thorns. If the stem is ripe, the thorn will snap off cleanly. If the thorn is soft and flexible, the stem is not yet ripe enough.

Make sure the knife you use is sharp and clean. Ragged cuts will not heal properly and could provide an entry point for disease.

If the union is a success, new growth will begin the following spring.

BUDDING

1 Cut a strong, ripe, healthy stem from the parent plant.

2 Trim off the leaves and snap off the thorns cleanly.

3 Hold the stem with its growing point toward you. Find a dormant bud and place the blade of the knife behind it. Draw the knife toward you to cut beneath the bud. Pull the knife to tear off a tail of bark (take great care not to cut yourself).

4 Pull off the pith behind the bud, using the knife if necessary.

5 Make a T-shaped cut in the rootstock, cutting no deeper than the bark. Ease back the bark with the tip of the knife.

6 Insert the bud into the cut on the rootstock, tail on top.

7 Then trim back the tail so it is level with the top of the T.

8 Bind the stem with a rubber tie and secure it with a pin. The rubber will stretch as the bud begins to swell and grow.

9 When the bud begins to grow strongly the following spring, remove the tie. Cut back the top growth of the rootstock and leave the rose as is for about a year.

SEMI-RIPE CUTTINGS

1 Select a side shoot that is still green but beginning to turn woody at the base. Cut just above an outward-facing bud.

2 Trim the cutting at the base, just below a leaf joint.

3 Trim back the soft tip to leave a length of stem about 4 inches long.

4 Remove the lower leaves and all the thorns, if any. Dip the base of the cutting in hormone rooting powder and tap off the excess.

5 Using a dibble, insert the cuttings up to two-thirds of their length in the rooting medium.

6 Firm the cuttings with your fingers, then spray them with a solution of copper fungicide both to moisten the soil mix and to kill off any fungal spores and bacteria.

Cuttings

Propagation of old roses is also possible by cuttings (semi-ripe or hardwood), but this technique is suitable only for very vigorous cultivars. Weaker-growing types are best increased by budding. Roses raised from cuttings have the advantage that suckers will be true to the parent. (Suckers on grafted plants will be from the rootstock.)

7 *(left)* Label the cuttings, then tent the pot with a plastic bag to prevent moisture loss. Support the bag with canes or wire hoops to prevent contact between the plastic and the leaves, because moisture will accumulate at that point and harbor bacteria. Keep the cuttings in a shady, frost-free place until rooted.

Semi-ripe cuttings

In very cold areas, you may have
more success with semi-ripe cuttings,
though these need more attention
both while rooting and when
overwintering. However, given
proper care, a higher proportion is
likelier to root by this method than
by hardwood cuttings.

Semi-ripe cuttings are taken from
mid- to late summer as the current
year's growth is beginning to ripen
and become woody. Root the cuttings
in pots containing an inert mixture of
peat and sharp sand. You need to
check the cuttings periodically.
Remove any fallen leaves that may
rot and make sure the rooting
medium stays fairly moist. Always
water with a fungicidal solution to
prevent the spread of fungi. Once the
cuttings have rooted (usually by the
following spring) they can be planted
out and grown on in nursery beds or
potted up individually, using loam-
based soil mix.

Hardwood cuttings

Most gardeners find taking hardwood
cuttings easiest, since it does not
require any special equipment and
the cuttings are taken in autumn

when roses experience an increase in
rooting activity. Furthermore,
aftercare is minimal.

Prepare a trench 9 inches to 1
foot deep in the open ground and
line it to one-third of its depth with
sharp sand.

Cut well-ripened, pencil-thick
stems from the rose, remove the soft
tip and trim to a length of about
9 inches, with the base cut just below
a leaf joint. Remove any leaves that
remain on the stem. Dip the base of

the cutting in hormone rooting
powder, then place it in the trench,
leaving about 3 inches above the soil
surface. Firm the cuttings in and
water well. If hard frosts cause soil
erosion, it may be necessary to re-firm
the cuttings during the winter.

The cuttings should be rooted by
the following autumn, when they can
be transferred to their final position
in the garden, if they are sufficiently
developed, or allowed to grow on for
another year.

Pests, diseases and other disorders

Most roses are prone to certain pests and diseases, but fortunately most of these are easy to control. Incidence of disease and pest attack depends to some extent on the climate and region. Black spot is more prevalent in some parts of the country than in others; for instance, mildew is more likely to be a problem if the weather is dry, and aphid populations will be affected to some extent by the winter survival of their predators.

Some rose varieties are more susceptible to problems than others, but well-fed roses that are growing strongly can usually survive any attack, provided you act quickly.

Maintaining good standards of garden hygiene decreases the likelihood and the severity of any problems. Regularly clear up any plant debris both from the roses and from other plants, as these may rot and harbor disease. You should also burn or otherwise dispose of any rose prunings (do not compost them) for the same reason. Make sure the plants have enough space around them to ensure good air circulation. You may need to rethink your planting scheme if they become overcrowded as they develop.

The following are some of the problems you are most likely to encounter in the garden. Systemic insecticides and fungicides are applied as a spray and are absorbed by the plant. They do not kill the pest or disease directly, so their effect is not immediate. Repeated applications are usually necessary.

Aphid

How to identify: The most common aphid to attack roses is the greenfly, usually spotted near the start of the season on the ends of stems and developing flowerbuds.
Cause: Failure to destroy prunings from the previous season that may harbor eggs. However, in practice this pest is virtually endemic and you are likely to encounter it every season.
Control: Spray the plants with a commercial systemic insecticide as soon as you notice an infestation and repeat as directed by the manufacturer. Some insecticides are selective in their action and leave beneficial insects such as ladybugs unharmed. Organic gardeners may spray with soft soap or use insecticide based on derris or pyrethrum. Though infestations may be heavy, the pest is easy to control and long-term damage can easily be avoided.

Aphid (Greenfly)

Balling

Balling

How to identify: Petals turn brown and cling together so the flowers fail to open properly.
Cause: Prolonged wet weather while the buds are developing. Aphid infestations earlier in the season can also lead to balling.
Control: None possible. Balling is a seasonal problem that does not affect the health of the plant overall, but you should remove balled flowers that may otherwise rot and allow diseases to take a hold. Roses with very delicate petals are the most susceptible, but ensuring they are planted where they will receive adequate drying sunlight will help minimize the risk of rain damage.

Black Spot

How to identify: Black spots or patches develop on the leaves and in some cases, the stems, from the middle of summer onward. The leaves yellow and eventually drop off. Plants left untreated will die back.
Cause: A bacterium that overwinters in the soil, then enters the plant during the growing season. Leaving infected prunings on the ground therefore increases the likelihood of its occurrence.
Control: Remove all infected leaves and stems and destroy them, then spray the plant with Bordeaux mixture. If you need to cut the plant hard back, feed and water well to encourage recovery. Blackspot is more common in certain geographical areas, and some

Black Spot

Mildew

Rust

Proliferation

rose varieties are more susceptible than others. In severe cases, replace with disease-resistant and guaranteed disease-free stock.

Powdery Mildew

How to identify: A whitish-gray powdering on the leaves and stems. If left untreated, the mildew could cover the whole plant.
Cause: Various fungi that thrive in dry soil and are most likely to cause damage where the air is warm, dry and stagnant.
Control: Spray with a commercial fungicide. Thin out congested growth. Where the overall planting is thick, and air circulation is therefore poor, replant to ensure more space around the plants.

Rust

How to identify: Orange spots that turn to black appear on the undersides of leaves from midsummer onward. If left untreated, rose rust can be fatal to the plant.
Cause: Fungal spores that are more prevalent in humid weather.
Control: Remove infected parts, then spray with a fungicide. Improve air circulation around the plants, as for mildew.

Dieback

How to identify: Flower buds, where present, do not mature and wither. Beginning at the tip of the stem, leaves begin to wither and drop off. The stem itself droops and may blacken.
Cause: Any of the diseases above, if not controlled, can

lead to dieback, but the condition may also be due to other fungi or bacteria, frost damage or a lack of soil nutrients, particularly potassium and phosphorus.
Control: Cut back all affected growth to clean, healthy wood, then feed the plant well. If dieback occurs in autumn, do not feed until the following spring, since any new growth you promote will itself be susceptible to winter frost damage.

Proliferation

How to identify: The stem continues to grow through the open flower, producing another bud or cluster of buds.
Cause: Damage to the stem while it is growing, either by frost or a virus.
Control: Cut off affected stems. If only a few stems are

affected, further steps are unnecessary, but where the whole plant has the condition a virus is probably the culprit and the whole plant will have to be dug up and destroyed.

Rose-sick soil

How to identify: The roses suddenly fail to thrive and begin to die back.
Cause: Complex and uncertain, but thought to be a combination of soil nutrient exhaustion with a build up of soil-borne nematodes, viruses and fungi. It usually occurs in ground that has supported roses for a number of years.
Control: It is best to replant new roses in soil that has not grown roses for at least seven years. Alternatively, dig up and discard the affected roses, replace the top 1 foot of soil and plant with fresh stock.

Calendar

Early spring

Improve the soil and plant new stock.
On established plants, cut out any
dead, diseased or damaged wood
(ideally once any danger of frost has
passed). Fork fertilizer around the base
of the roses as growth emerges, water
in well and mulch. Cut back the
rootstock on roses that were budded
during the previous summer and that
are showing signs of fresh growth.

Mid- to late spring

Check for and begin control of aphid
infestations. Plant new stock.

Midsummer

Deadhead repeat-flowering roses and
any others not grown for their
decorative hips. Trim hedges after
flowering (unless grown for their
hips). Thin twiggy growth on gallicas
to improve air circulation. Feed all
roses after pruning. Increase your
stock by taking semi-ripe cuttings
(vigorous types only) or by budding.
Check for and control black spot, rust
and mildew. Plant new stock
(container-grown only).

Late summer

Peg down stems of hybrid perpetuals
and other types that produce long
flexible stems. Tie in strong new
shoots on roses trained as climbers.
Continue to take semi-ripe cuttings
of vigorous plants.

Autumn

Fork in bonemeal around the base of
the plants, water in well and mulch.
Plant new stock. Take hardwood
cuttings of vigorous roses.

Late winter

Tidy up hedges, such as *Rosa rugosa*,
that have ornamental hips and were
thus not pruned after flowering. In
frosty weather, if the soil surface
freezes and cracks open, firm in
hardwood cuttings.

■ RIGHT
A hedge of *Rosa rugosa* caught in late
summer. The tomato-like hips redden as
the season advances until, in autumn, they
provide a display to match that of the
summer flowers.

Other recommended roses

In addition to the roses illustrated in the gallery section, the following are recommended. The date of introduction follows the name of the rose in parentheses. The dimensions of the rose under good growing conditions are given at the end of the description, the first figure indicating the rose's final height, the second its spread.

'**Andersonii**' (uncertain) *canina* hybrid. Deep pink, lightly scented, single flowers appear in early summer. 8 feet x 8 feet.

'**Ballerina**' (1937) Polyantha. Pink, lightly scented, single flowers, carried in clusters throughout summer, have white centers. 4 feet x 4 feet.

'**Blanche Double de Coubert**' (1892) Rugosa shrub. White, sweetly scented, semidouble flowers open flat from pointed, pinkish buds from summer to autumn. 5 feet x 4 feet.

'**Bloomfield Abundance**' (1920) China. Delicate soft pink, lightly scented, double flowers open from buds with long, feathery calyces from summer to autumn. 6 feet x 5 feet.

'**Blush Damask**' (uncertain) Damask. Deep lilac pink, sweetly scented, fully double flowers are produced in midsummer. 4 feet x 4 feet or more.

'**Caimaieux**' (1830) Gallica. Fragrant, fully double, white flowers, produced in midsummer, are striped and splashed with crimson. 4 feet x 3 feet.

'**Celsiana**' (before 1750) Damask. Deep rose pink, strongly fragrant, semidouble flowers are borne in clusters in midsummer. 5 feet x 4 feet.

x *centifolia* (uncertain) Centifolia. Soft pink, heavily scented, fully double flowers are produced in midsummer. 5 feet x 5 feet.

x *centifolia* '**Cristata**' (1820) Centifolia. Warm pink, sweetly scented, fully double flowers emerge from 'tricorn' buds during midsummer. 5 feet x 4 feet.

'**Chianti**' (1967) Modern shrub. Deep crimson, richly fragrant, fully double flowers that age to purple are carried in midsummer. 5 feet x 5 feet.

'**Commandant Beaurepaire**' (1874) Bourbon. Deep pink, fragrant, double flowers, splashed and striped with purple, maroon and paler pink, appear in midsummer and, sporadically, in autumn. 6 feet x 5 feet.

'**Common Moss**' (around 1696) Moss. Clear pink, fragrant, fully double flowers are borne in midsummer. 5 feet x 5 feet.

■ RIGHT
'Bloomfield Abundance'

'Comte de Chambord' (1860)
Portland. Deep pink, sweetly scented,
fully double flowers are produced
in summer and again in autumn.
4 feet x 4 feet.

'Comtesse du Cayla' (1902) China.
Copper-orange, fragrant, semidouble
flowers that fade to salmon pink are
produced from summer to autumn.
5 feet x 5 feet.

'Cornelia' (1925) Hybrid musk.
Double, sweetly scented flowers,
carried from summer to autumn, fade
from apricot-pink to creamy pink.
5 feet x 5 feet.

'De Meaux' (1789) Centifolia. Soft
pink, sweetly scented, fully double
flowers appear in midsummer.
3 feet x 3 feet.

'De Rescht' (uncertain) Damask.
Deep magenta-red, heavily scented,
fully double flowers appear in
midsummer, then intermittently until
autumn. 3 feet x 3 feet.

eglanteria Wild rose. Pink, lightly
scented, single flowers are carried
amid fragrant leaves in midsummer
and are followed by scarlet hips.
8 feet x 8 feet.

'Empereur du Maroc' (1858) Hybrid
perpetual. Crimson, intensely
fragrant, fully double flowers appear
in midsummer and autumn.
4 feet x 3 feet.

'Empress Josephine' (uncertain)
Gallica. Bright pink, lightly scented,
loosely double flowers, veined with
deeper pink, are produced in
midsummer. 4 feet x 4 feet.

'Felicia' (1928) Modern shrub. Pale
pink, sweetly scented, fully double
flowers are carried from summer to
autumn. 5 feet x 7 feet.

'Ferdinand Pichard' (1921) Bourbon.
Deep pink, richly scented, loosely
double flowers, striped with crimson
and purple, appear from midsummer
to autumn. 4 feet x 4 feet.

foetida Wild rose. Bright yellow,
unpleasantly scented, single
flowers are borne in early summer.
5 feet x 5 feet.

'Frau Karl Druschki' (1901) Hybrid
perpetual. Pure white, scentless, fully
double flowers emerge from pink-

tinted buds in mid- and late summer.
4 feet x 4 feet.

'Fru Dagmar Hastrup' (1914)
Rugosa. Light pink, strongly scented,
single flowers are borne in summer
and autumn. 3 feet x 4 feet.

'Frühlingsmorgen' (1941) Modern
shrub. Creamy white, lightly scented,
single flowers are carried in late
spring. 6 feet x 5 feet.

'Général Kléber' (1850s) Moss. Soft
pink, fragrant, fully double flowers
with a silky sheen are carried in
midsummer. 5 feet x 5 feet.

'Georg Arends' (1910) Hybrid
perpetual. Soft rose-pink, fragrant,

■ LEFT
R. moyesii

sporadically, in autumn.
6 feet x 8 feet.
'Madame Pierre Oger' (1878)
Bourbon. Pale silvery pink, sweetly
scented, fully double flowers are
produced from summer to autumn.
6 feet x 4 feet.
'Mousseline' (1855) Moss.
Soft flesh-pink to creamy white,
fragrant, semidouble flowers are
produced in midsummer.
To 4 feet x 4 feet.
moyesii Wild rose. Crimson,
virtually scentless, single flowers
appear from early summer to
midsummer, followed in autumn
by brilliant scarlet hips. 8 feet x 5
feet. 'Geranium' is a popular
cultivar.
'Mrs. John Laing' (1887) Hybrid
perpetual. Silvery pink, sweetly
scented, fully double flowers are
freely produced from summer to
autumn. 3 feet x 3 feet.
'Old Blush China' (around 1750 in
Europe, but grown in China
possibly from the 10th century or
earlier) China. Pale pink, lightly
scented, double flowers are
produced from summer to autumn.
3 feet x 3 feet.
'Penelope' (1924) Modern shrub.
Pale pink, sweetly scented,
semidouble flowers are borne from
summer to autumn. 3 feet x 3 feet.
'Perle d'Or' (1883) China. Pale
pink, sweetly scented, double
flowers appear from summer to
autumn. 4 feet x 3 feet.

fully double flowers appear
from mid- to late summer.
6 feet x 6 feet.
'Gertrude Jekyll' (1986) 'English'
rose. Deep pink, very fragrant,
fully double flowers are carried from
summer to autumn.
5 feet x 3 feet.
'Gloire de France' (1819) Gallica.
Pale mauve-pink, very fragrant, fully
double flowers appear in midsummer.
3 feet x 3 feet.
'Golden Wings' (1956) Modern
shrub. Pale golden yellow, lightly
scented, single flowers are
produced throughout summer.
3 feet x 4 feet or more.
'Great Maiden's Blush' (15th
century or earlier) Alba. Soft pink,
sweetly scented, double flowers
appear in midsummer or later.

5 feet x 5 feet or more.
'Heritage' (1984) 'English' rose.
Apricot-pink, strongly scented,
fully double flowers are produced
from summer to autumn.
4 feet x 4 feet.
'Jacques Cartier' (1866) Bourbon.
Clear pink, strongly scented, fully
double flowers are paler at the edges
and are borne in summer and
again, but unreliably, in autumn.
4 feet x 3 feet.
'Lady Hillingdon' (1910) Tea.
Apricot-yellow, fragrant, semi-double
flowers open from copper-orange
buds from summer until autumn or
later. 2^1/$_2$ feet x 2 feet.
'Marguerite Hilling' (1959) Modern
shrub. Pale pink, lightly scented,
semidouble flowers appear in
midsummer and again,

■ BELOW
'The Fairy'

'**Pink Grootendorst**' (1923) Rugosa. Carnation-like, pale pink, scentless, double flowers have fimbriated (fringed) edges and are produced from summer to autumn. 6 feet x 5 feet.

primula Wild rose. Pale yellow, lightly scented, single flowers appear in late spring. The leaves are aromatic when wet. 6 feet x 6 feet.

'**Reine des Violettes**' (1860) Hybrid perpetual. Deep red, heavily scented, fully double flowers, aging to dove gray, are produced from summer to autumn. 6 feet x 6 feet.

'**Reine Victoria**' (1872) Bourbon. Rose pink, sweetly scented, fully double flowers are produced from summer to autumn. 6 feet x 4 feet.

'**Sombreuil**' (1850) Tea. Cream, fragrant, double flowers, flushed pink, appear from summer to autumn. 4 feet x 4 feet.

'**Souvenir du Docteur Jamain**' (1865) Hybrid perpetual. Wine-red, fragrant, fully double flowers are carried in summer and autumn. 6 feet x 6 feet.

'**St Nicholas**' (uncertain) Damask. Rich pink, fragrant, semidouble flowers appear in midsummer. 4 feet x 4 feet.

'**The Bishop**' (uncertain) Centifolia. Cerise-purple, fragrant, fully double flowers appear in midsummer then fade to lilac-mauve. 5 feet x 3 feet.

'**The Fairy**' (1932) Polyantha. Pale pink, scentless, double flowers are freely produced in clusters from late summer to late autumn. 2 feet x 2 feet or more.

'**Tour de Malakoff**' (1856) Centifolia. Produces rich magenta-purple, heavily scented, fully double, cupped flowers in midsummer that age to dove gray. 6 feet x 5 feet.

'**Variegata di Bologna**' (1909) Bourbon. Pale lilac-pink, heavily scented, fully double flowers, striped with intense crimson-purple, appear in midsummer and autumn. To 6 feet x 6 feet.

'**Viridiflora**' (before 1833) China. Curious, green, scentless, double 'flowers' (actually modified leaves) are produced from summer to autumn. 3 feet x 2 feet.

Index

ACKNOWLEDGMENTS
The pictures on pages 13, 16, 43 and 49b were lent by Peter McHoy.